ihe Sierra Club
book of our na-

917.304 Young, Donald
YOU   The Sierra Club book of
         our national parks

11A5358

ihe Sierra Club
book of our na-
tional parks

BRODART   05/92   14.95

DATE	BORROWER'S NAME	
OCT 03 199		

The Sierra Club Book of
Our National Parks

Defying gravity, Double Arch bakes in the hot sun. It's just one of the more than 90 rock formations that make Arches National Park unique.

The still waters of a Snake River beaver pond mirror the snowy peaks that crown Grand Teton National Park.

The Sierra Club Book of
Our National Parks

Donald Young
with Cynthia Overbeck Bix

Sierra Club Books | Little, Brown and Company
San Francisco | Boston • Toronto • London

The Sierra Club, founded in 1892 by John Muir, has devoted itself to the study and protection of the earth's scenic and ecological resources — mountains, wetlands, woodlands, wild shores and rivers, deserts and plains. The publishing program of the Sierra Club offers books to the public as a nonprofit educational service in the hope that they may enlarge the public's understanding of the Club's basic concerns. The Sierra Club has some sixty chapters in the United States and in Canada. For information about how you may participate in its programs to preserve wilderness and the quality of life, please address inquiries to Sierra Club, 730 Polk Street, San Francisco, CA 94109.

Text copyright © 1990 by Donald Young and Cynthia Overbeck Bix

First Edition

10 9 8 7 6 5 4 3 2 1

Sierra Club Books/Little, Brown children's books are published by Little, Brown and Company (Inc.) in association with Sierra Club Books.

Published simultaneously in Canada by Little, Brown & Company (Canada) Limited

Printed in Hong Kong

Photo Credits
© Chip Clark: 37; © Peter French: 9; © Steven Fuller: 41; © Jeff Gnass: 34, 38; © Jeff Gnass/West Stock: 42; © John Hendrickson: 44; © Lewis Kemper: 40; © Dave Martin: 49; © Buddy Mays: 33; © David Muench: 2, 7, 10, 11; National Park Service Photographic Collection: 16, 20, 26, 29, 30; Photographic Archives of the Arkansas State University Museum: 19; The Sierra Club William E. Colby Memorial Library Collection: 21, 22, 25, 47; U.S. Department of the Interior, Grand Canyon National Park: 27; Utah State Historical Society; 17; © Art Wolfe: 8; Yosemite NPS Research Library: 50; © Donald Young: 1, 12, 14, 43.

Design: Williams + Ziller Design

Library of Congress Catalog Card Number 89-60740

Library of Congress Cataloging-in-Publication Data

Young, Donald.
    The Sierra Club book of our national parks / Donald Young with Cynthia Overbeck Bix.
        p.   cm.
    Includes index.
    Summary: Describes the history, attractions, and diversity of a number of national parks, including the Grand Canyon, Maine's Acadia National Park, and Alaska's Gates of the Arctic National Park and Preserve.
    ISBN 0-316-97744-6
    1. National parks and reserves — United States — Juvenile literature.   [1. National parks and reserves.]   I. Overbeck, Cynthia.   II. Title.   III. Title: Our national parks.
E160.Y66   1990
917.304′927 — dc20   89-60740
                                                            CIP
                                                            AC

Contents

Our Beautiful Land   6
MOUNTAINS • FORESTS • DESERTS • CANYONS • RIVERS • LAKES • HISTORIC SITES

The Beginnings of the Park System   15
EXPLORERS • SETTLERS • EXPLOITERS • TOURISTS • PRESERVATIONISTS

At One with Nature   32
CAMPING • HIKING • BOATING • SWIMMING • SKIING • SNOWSHOEING • BIRDING

Facing the Future   45
DEVELOPMENT • POLLUTION • OVERCROWDING • EXPANSION • PROTECTION

Map of U.S. National Parks   52

List of U.S. National Parks   54
AREAS • FEATURES • ACTIVITIES

Index   63

Our Beautiful Land

Early on a summer morning, just after dawn, you pause on the rocky, zigzagging trail you're hiking and look around you. The trail is carved into the steep wall of an enormous canyon. Walls and towers of rock rise on either side, as far as you can see. Across from you, 10 miles away, the cliffs look like great rock temples, painted gold and pink by the rising sun. You take a deep breath of the cool, pine-scented air. Everything is perfectly silent.

Suddenly, a big black raven swoops off the cliff above you and soars out over the canyon. Your stomach flutters as you see the immense drop beneath the bird. It's a full mile down to the river that winds like a narrow silver ribbon below.

That river helped to carve out this canyon, inch by inch, over millions of years. If you hike all the way to the bottom, the path will take you on a jour-ney backward in time, through 2 billion years of geological history. Each colorful layer of rock is like a chapter in the story, from the most recent layers, at the top, down to some of the oldest exposed rock in the world, at the bottom.

Along the way, you will find fossils — remains or imprints of seashells and small marine animals — imbedded in the rock. They come from a time, millions of years ago, when this land was actually under a prehistoric sea. Today, the canyon is alive with animals and plants of every description. On your hike you will come across everything from dwarf piñon pines to cactus, and from scampering chipmunks to bighorn sheep.

Where on earth is this spectacular scene? By now you've probably guessed that it's in Arizona's Grand Canyon National Park, the site of one of the greatest natural wonders of the world.

Sheer cliffs and colorful rock formations make the Grand Canyon a place of unequaled beauty. At Toroweap Point, the canyon wall drops a dizzying 3,000 feet straight down.

Whether you hike down into the canyon or just sit quietly under a pine tree to look and listen, you will certainly appreciate the beauty of this special place.

What you may not realize is that it took the efforts of many dedicated people to preserve this unique area. In the past, the Grand Canyon, like many other beautiful places, has been threatened with change and even destruction by "progress." In the 1800s, for example, some people tried to establish ore mining operations in the canyon. And as recently as 1963, people proposed a dam that would have flooded 150 of the canyon's 277 miles with water. This would have hidden the lower part of the colorful walls and drowned countless plants and animal habitats.

Fortunately, some citizens have always realized the value of keeping at least a portion of our vast and beautiful land in as close to a natural state as possible. We all need a place to which we can escape from the noise and pressures of city and suburban life. We need to preserve areas with fresh air and open space, where we can wander along a forest stream, or camp out under the stars, or watch a doe and her fawn drink from a mountain lake. Some places, like the Grand Canyon, also deserve protection because they contain scenery, plants, or animals found nowhere else in the world.

The national parks were created to protect our nation's precious and irreplaceable land. The Grand Canyon is one of the most famous, but many other parks, monuments, and historical sites make up the National Park System. Each has its own special value and significance. Of the more than 350 large and small sites in the system, 50 are *national*

An escape to the quiet beauty of a place like Olympic National Park rewards a visitor with visual delights such as this black-tailed fawn among the wildflowers.

Red-hot lava shoots skyward at Puu o Keokeo in Hawaii Volcanoes National Park. A volcanic eruption is just one of the many dramatic natural events that take place in our national parks.

parks. For the most part, these are large areas, often with many acres preserved in a near-wilderness state. National parks contain many kinds of landscapes, from islands to beaches to mountains. Often, a special feature of the landscape is the biggest or most perfect example of its kind. In Alaska's Denali National Park and Preserve, for example, Mount McKinley towers 20,320 feet, to be the highest mountain in North America. In Redwood National Park, California, the tallest tree in the world, a coast redwood, rises 367.8 feet from its perch on the edge of a stream. And beneath the green forests of Kentucky, in Mammoth Cave National Park, extends the world's longest known cave system. In its 300 miles of mapped passages, colorful mineral formations and strange blind creatures create an underground wonderland.

In addition to the highest mountain, the tallest tree, and the longest cave system, our national parks preserve unusual landscape features that may be found nowhere else in the world. The variety in the parks is dazzling. In Alaska's Glacier Bay National Park and Preserve, you can stand on the deck of a boat and see "living" glaciers looming in frozen majesty above the blue bay. Hawaii Volcanoes National Park contains active volcanoes, and, if you're

Now silent and abandoned, the magnificent Cliff Palace in Mesa Verde National Park was home to Native Americans many centuries ago.

lucky, you can watch an actual eruption, complete with fiery molten lava shooting skyward. And in Yellowstone National Park, Old Faithful and other geysers regularly erupt like volcanoes of boiling water, sending jets of steam into the air.

The handiwork of humans, not nature, is the attraction at Mesa Verde National Park, in Colorado. There you can climb to a fabulous city of stone dwellings built in the cliffs by Native American people 800 years ago.

Many parks were created to protect the unique wildlife and plants living there. In Florida's Everglades National Park, thousands of snowy egrets, great egrets, and pink-winged roseate spoonbills — and more than 300 other bird species — populate the ponds, mangrove forests, and saw-grass prairies. Shenandoah National Park, in the Blue Ridge Mountains of Virginia, preserves dense, leafy hardwood forests of hemlock, oak, and birch that once blanketed much of the East Coast. And in Rocky Mountain National Park, Colorado, the fragile alpine tundra contains such unique plants as 3-inch-high dwarf clover that may be up to 200 years old!

The national parks are the most spectacular and well-known of the areas in the National Park System. But the system also includes many other, smaller sites. Nearly 80 of these are *national monuments*. These are usually designated to protect a single distinctive kind of plant or other landscape feature. For example, Wyoming's unique Devil's Tower is an 865-foot pillar of rock created by an ancient volcanic eruption and millions of years of erosion. Arizona's Organ Pipe Cactus National Monument protects rare cacti

Among nature's living marvels are these prickly giants, protected at Organ Pipe Cactus National Monument.

A beautiful fall day is the perfect time to enjoy the Delaware Water Gap National Recreation Area — one of the many NRAs included in the park system.

having huge vertical arms, sometimes 20 feet tall or more, that grow in clusters resembling organ pipes. And Dinosaur National Monument, in Utah and Colorado, is a treasure trove of dinosaur bones — the world's richest fossil deposit of prehistoric giants.

Other national monuments preserve important aspects of human culture. For example, Alabama's Russell Cave National Monument contains tools, weapons, and human bones that prove people lived in its spooky passageways for some 8,000 years.

Other areas preserved under the National Park System include those that offer recreational activities in beautiful natural surroundings. *National seashores*, such as North Carolina's Cape Hatteras National Seashore, and *national lakeshores*, like Pictured Rocks National Lakeshore in Michigan, are special places where you can enjoy the water as well as the scenery. *National wild and scenic rivers*, such as Alaska's Alagnak Wild River and Wisconsin's lovely Saint Croix National Scenic Riverway, offer opportunities for either whitewater rafting or peaceful boating.

National scenic trails, like the East's

2,100-mile Appalachian National Scenic Trail, offer long-distance footpaths through unspoiled park areas. And *national recreation areas*, such as New York's Gateway NRA and Glen Canyon NRA in Utah and Arizona, are usually set aside for water recreation, either in a natural or an urban setting. Although much other beautiful land is also preserved in national forests, national wildlife refuges, and state parks, these are not part of the National Park System.

In addition to protecting natural landscapes, wildlife, and plants, the National Park System protects our cultural heritage. Some national monuments are set aside for this purpose: the Statue of Liberty National Monument is one shining example. *National historic sites, national historical parks*, and *national battlefields* also preserve the places where people important to U.S. history have lived and worked or where historic events have occurred.

Our national parklands are remarkable in their variety and beauty. From the immense depths of the Grand Canyon to the icy summits of Alaska's Wrangell–St. Elias mountain ranges, the park system contains every imaginable kind of landscape, plant, and animal. But the story of the parks is the story of people, too — those who would exploit or destroy these wonders as well as those who would preserve them. As the history of the national parks unfolds in the next chapter, you will come to appreciate the foresight and dedication that were necessary to establish the system we enjoy today.

In early spring, a delicate mist hangs over the green hilltops of Shenandoah National Park's beautiful Blue Ridge Mountains.

The Beginnings of the Park System

Land! That's something the United States always had plenty of. Rolling hills and wide meadows, craggy mountains and green forests stretch across the continent, from the Atlantic to the Pacific oceans. Today, the amount of land still in its natural, unspoiled state is relatively small. But when the first European settlers stepped from their wooden ships into the New World in the early 1600s, they found a vast wilderness. The new land was thick with forests and alive with countless birds and wild animals.

Although tribes of Native Americans had lived on the land for centuries, they had scarcely made a mark. Theirs was a simple culture, and they lived lightly on the land. They hunted only the animals they needed for food and skins and cleared only small bits of land for growing crops.

But the Europeans had different ideas about land. They had come from countries like England and the Netherlands, where almost all land had been altered by humans to meet their needs. They needed cleared land, not forests, for their farms. They wanted to grow the foods they were used to eating, flax and cotton to spin cloth for their clothes, and crops to feed their sheep, horses, and cattle. Many of them had come to the New World to make a new start, or even to make their fortunes. When they looked at the forest wilderness, they saw an obstacle, not a thing of beauty. To them, beauty meant something else: cattle grazing peacefully, smoke curling from a cabin chimney, plowed land planted with corn and other crops. The idea of preserving nature would have seemed frivolous to most of those hard-working pioneers. Besides, there was still plenty more of it beyond their clearings!

15

For hundreds of years, loggers chopped away at forests all across the East. Here, in Tennessee's Great Smoky Mountains, ox teams haul huge logs that were felled using nothing more than hand axes.

So down came the trees. For the next 300 years, one of the most familiar sounds echoing across America was the "thunk" of an axe striking a tree. Trees provided the logs for cabins, the boards for churches and village shops, and fuel for the stoves and fireplaces in every structure. As time went by, the trees also fueled factories that manufactured goods of all kinds, from cloth to plows.

The cleared land became farms or grazing pastures for livestock. Roads crisscrossed the land, and docks went up on bays and rivers. Gradually, the forests that had seemed limitless began to shrink, and the edge of the wilderness was pushed farther west.

While the East was fast becoming "civilized," much of the land west of the Mississippi River was still untamed. Out there were massive, rugged landscapes, wilder than anything most of the Europeans had seen. The Rocky Mountains were more extensive than any mountains in Europe. The canyons were so deep that it was hard to hear the roar of the rivers far below. The Southwest was vast and dry, dotted with strange spiny plants and unusual rock formations.

In the mid-1800s, the few hardy men who explored and mapped the West came upon unimagined scenic wonders. Many of these explorers judged the land from a strictly practical point of view. They were looking for new land to settle, and grand, rugged scenery wasn't much good for farming. In 1857, a U.S. surveying party led by Lt. Joseph Ives traveled up the Colorado River to what we now call the Grand Canyon. Although Ives thought the scenery beautiful, he could not believe anyone else would want to visit it. "The region is, of course, altogether valueless," he wrote in his report to the government. "Ours has been the first, and will doubtless be the last, party of whites to visit this profitless locality." Seldom has a prediction been so wrong!

Other explorers, however, reacted with more foresight to what they saw. Major John Wesley Powell, the daring one-armed ex-soldier who led one of the last great western exploring parties, was deeply impressed. In 1869, Powell and his men determined to ride the

The brave one-armed explorer John Wesley Powell consults with a Paiute Indian guide. In 1869, Powell led an expedition through the dangerous canyons of the Green and Colorado rivers.

17

Green and Colorado rivers from Wyoming through the wild, unknown country of Utah and Arizona, into the Grand Canyon and beyond. Much of that country was unexplored, and for many miles its rivers became dangerous whitewater rapids crashing through deep gorges. Powell and his men risked starvation and drowning. At one point, Powell called the treacherous water "a wild beast." Yet when he climbed one steep canyon wall and viewed the rocky spires and buttes of what is now Utah's Canyonlands National Park, he called it "a world of grandeur." Powell felt that such a land was worth risking a great deal to see.

At about the same time, people were debating the creation of the very first national park, in an area of the Rocky Mountains known then simply as "Wonderland." Until then, no one had ever created a national park anywhere in the world. In Europe, there were public gardens in cities, where people could enjoy a pleasant stroll along tree-lined paths or small city lakes. And larger areas of privately owned land were set aside by kings and wealthy men as their personal hunting or pleasure grounds. But nowhere was a large, unspoiled area of land set aside by a national government for all citizens to enjoy.

A small, early step toward establishing the principle that natural landscape features were worth preserving had been taken by the U.S. government in 1832. In that year, Congress had approved the creation of the Hot Springs Reservation in Arkansas. There, 47 natural hot springs welled up from deep underground. The water from those springs was believed to be good for various illnesses, so people flocked there to bathe in the steaming waters.

But Hot Springs was hardly preserved in its natural state. A town, complete with hotels, bathhouses, and shops, was built over and around the springs. By the late 1800s, the water was flowing to the bathhouses along Hot Springs Creek, which was channeled through pipes under the main street. Though the site, which is now a national park, includes pretty tree-shaded trails, it looks nothing like the wilderness parks that were created later.

The first of these, the area that stirred people to think of a national park for the first time, was "Wonderland" — a spectacular segment of Rocky Mountain wilderness that we now call Yellowstone National Park. It was explored as far back as 1807 by John Colter, a former member of the Lewis and Clark expedition. He and the other trappers, gold prospectors, and "mountain men" who followed him reported amazing sights. They described smoking plumes of gases, or fumaroles; geysers shooting hot water hundreds of feet in the air; and swirling, rainbow-colored pools of mineral waters.

People in the East thought these were just "tall tales." But a curious U.S. government finally sent an official expedition into the region in 1870. That group of civilians, escorted by the U.S.

Maybe a soak in hot mineral waters will ease their aches and pains! These nineteenth-century ladies are giving it a try at Arkansas' Hot Springs Reservation, one of the first natural landscape features to be preserved.

Cavalry, gazed in wonder at Yellowstone Falls, Yellowstone Lake, and the geysers. One remarkable geyser "performed" on such a predictable schedule that they named it "Old Faithful."

The men immediately recognized how special the region was, but they disagreed about what to do with it. One night around their campfire, several said they intended to stake claims around the geysers and charge tourists money to see them. But a more farsighted man named Cornelius Hedges argued that the area "ought to be set apart as a great National Park," protected from exploitation for all to enjoy.

One of his campfire companions, Nathaniel P. Langford, spent the next few months publicizing the region and urging Congress to approve a park there.

In 1872, Congress did pass a law creating Yellowstone National Park — the first of its kind. The law described Yellowstone as "a public park or pleasuring ground for the benefit and enjoyment of the people." Along with the reports of the government expeditions, what had helped convince Congress to act was the powerful Northern Pacific Railroad. The rail company saw the park as a big money-making opportunity. It extended rail lines so that tour-

19

ists could get to the new park easily, and built tourist hotels.

In 1886, the U.S. Army was given responsibility for "policing" the park, as well as for managing the forests and wildlife. But, unfortunately, wildlife management was not well understood in those days. Most people believed that the land was made for the benefit of humanity. So naturally, the army did its job with people, not animals, in mind. There was little knowledge of the "balance of nature": that many species of plants and animals are interdependent

in ways that we do not fully understand. The park guardians did not realize that disturbing one species would affect others in unpredictable — and sometimes disastrous — ways.

For example, the army assumed that grazing animals such as deer and elk were what the tourists came to see. So they became overly protective of those animals. They killed off the wolves, coyotes, and mountain lions that hunted them. As a result, the elk and deer multiplied and soon had consumed all of their food supply. It became necessary

Mammoth Hotel, one of Yellowstone National Park's first, received guests arriving by horse-drawn coach in grand style.

John Muir, champion of the wilderness preservation movement, was a deeply thoughtful writer and philosopher as well as a daring mountaineer.

from time to time to consider killing them, to prevent mass starvation. The managers of the land meant well, but they had many lessons to learn about not upsetting nature's balance.

The science of conservation and the idea of preservation were not yet widely established in the United States. No one voice had yet spoken out for protection of the land in its unspoiled state. But a few early thinkers had recognized the importance of wilderness land. The great writer Henry David Thoreau thought Americans were losing something very valuable as they continued to chop down forests. In 1851 he wrote the now-famous words "In wildness is the preservation of the world." He was convinced that opportunities to enjoy the ruggedness of nature would make all people stronger in body and spirit.

But the great spokesman of the preservation movement came forward in the late 1800s. His name was John Muir, and his fight to preserve Yosemite Valley in California provided the basis for the philosophy of the park system as we know it today.

John Muir was a remarkable man whose passion for wilderness ruled every aspect of his long, productive life. His energy and daring in the mountains made him a legend in his own lifetime. His writings expressed a love of nature that has inspired generations. And his untiring crusade to preserve the wilderness in Yosemite and other regions led to a series of national parks all over the West.

Muir was born in Scotland in 1838 and came to Wisconsin with his family at the age of eleven. A lover of the outdoors

21

The greatest cause in Muir's life was the magnificent area now preserved as Yosemite National Park. Here, he admires his beloved Yosemite Valley.

from childhood, he studied geology and botany at the University of Wisconsin. Through his studies, he discovered an order and harmony in nature. In wilderness untouched by humans, everything seemed to fit together. The young Muir saw in nature a grand design created by God, and this philosophy carried him through his career as a naturalist and park crusader.

Muir was never one to do the expected thing. He dropped out of college and in 1867, at the age of twenty-nine, struck out all alone to hike from Indiana to the Gulf of Mexico, 1,000 miles away. A lean man with a long, shaggy beard and piercing blue eyes, he must have been a strange figure as he wandered through forests or turned up occasionally in towns.

Next, Muir headed west, to San Francisco, California. He quickly left that city and plunged into the wilderness of the Sierra Nevada. There he found his beloved Yosemite Valley and the cause that would become his life's work.

Muir first saw Yosemite Valley in 1868. From that day, he devoted himself to it with an almost religious passion. Since then, millions of people who have seen Yosemite have shared Muir's belief that this 7-mile-long valley is one of the most beautiful areas in the United States. The tall, light gray granite walls rise steeply from the valley floor. The immense rocks were roughly carved and scoured by mighty glaciers during the Ice Age, yet they look perfectly designed, as if by some great sculptor. In the spring, as the snow melts in the high mountains, several waterfalls tumble hundreds of feet to the valley floor. Deer and other animals roam through the broad grassy meadows, past the Merced River, which flows swiftly out of the mountains.

Muir also loved the vast, rugged mountain country that rose around the valley. He took off into the mountains at every opportunity, on dangerous solo hikes and climbs that earned him the nickname "John O'Mountains."

Muir left Yosemite temporarily when marriage, children, and a growing career as a writer of articles took him in other directions. But in the late 1870s he was back. Although the valley area had been a California state park for several years, it had been badly mismanaged. Inside the park, ramshackle hotels, shops, and saloons had been built. In the high country, sheep and cattle ranged freely, trampling the meadows and gobbling up vast quantities of wildflowers and other plants. And lumbermen were illegally cutting down trees.

Something had to be done. In the spring of 1889, Muir went camping in Yosemite with an old friend, Robert Underwood Johnson. Johnson was the influential editor of a popular magazine that had published some of Muir's articles. Although the two men felt the valley was beyond help, they hoped to save the high country around it. Johnson suggested that Muir write articles proposing that the federal land around the valley be made a national preserve, like Yellowstone, and called Yosemite National Park.

In his writing, Muir wanted to convince the public of the importance of experiencing wilderness as well as to crusade for its preservation by the government. His beautiful, emotional appeal struck a deep chord in many readers. "Climb the mountains and get their good tidings," he wrote. "Nature's peace will flow into you as the sunshine into the trees. The winds will blow their freshness into you, and the storms their energy, while cares will drop off like autumn leaves."

Muir's message arrived at just the right time in America's history. During the last decades of the nineteenth century, people were crowded into large cities that got dirtier and noisier every year. Out in the open countryside, the effects of industry, cattle and sheep ranching, and the lumber business were beginning to scar the land. People were becoming aware of problems caused by erosion and pollution. Many species of plants and animals were becoming rare or even disappearing for good. People began to see that in their rush to make money and acquire goods, they were destroying something irreplaceable.

Not only that, but they were losing touch with an important part of themselves as human beings. As Muir wrote, "Thousands of tired, nerve-shaken, over-civilized people are beginning to find out that going to the mountains is going home; that wildness is a necessity;

and that mountain parks and reservations are useful not only as fountains of timber and irrigating rivers, but as fountains of life."

In 1890, the federal land surrounding Yosemite Valley was made a national park by Congress. Sixteen years later, control of the valley was transferred from the state of California to the federal government, thereby completing the park. The efforts of Muir and Johnson on behalf of Yosemite are an early example of how the dedication and energy of individuals can make all the difference in the creation of a national park.

At the turn of the century the first national park in Oregon was created through the efforts of another tireless individual, William Gladstone Steel. His dedication to the cause of Crater Lake began in childhood, when he read an article in a newspaper his mother had wrapped around his school lunch. The article described a beautiful lake high in the mountains of Oregon, which had been formed in a crater left by an enormous volcanic explosion some 7,000 years ago.

Though Steel lived in Kansas, far from the West Coast, he decided he had to visit that lake. Many years later, in 1885, he finally stood in wonder at its rim. Then and there he decided that it must be protected as a national park. He spent the next 17 years lobbying and lecturing, trying to convince Congress. In 1902 his efforts paid off, and Crater Lake National Park was approved.

Around the same time, a pioneer naturalist named Enos Mills was fighting for a park in the Colorado Rocky Mountains. From the age of fourteen he had guided tourists on mountain hikes there. Mills had long believed that a national park should be created to protect the Front Range, from Longs Peak to Pikes Peak. He knew the area well and loved it deeply; during his lifetime, he actually climbed 14,225-foot Longs Peak 296 times! Inspired by John Muir, he spent years crusading for the creation of a park. Finally, in 1915, Congress established Rocky Mountain National Park.

All this time, the preservation movement was gaining momentum. But though the efforts of individuals were effective, organization was needed. As early as 1889, Muir's friend Robert Underwood Johnson had suggested that an organization of private citizens could help preserve the land in Yosemite and other parts of California. Muir welcomed the idea of a club that could "do something for wildness and make the mountains glad." Along with some professors from the University of California and Stanford University, Muir formed the Sierra Club in 1892. He was elected president, a position he held until his death in 1914. From the beginning, Sierra Club members explored the outdoors, often in outings organized by the club. At first, members were con-

Early Sierra Club members hear an enthusiastic lecture on nature's wonders from their founder and president, John Muir.

centrated in California and were concerned mainly with protecting the Sierra Nevada region. But today, the club's hundreds of thousands of members spread across the United States and Canada are concerned with a wide variety of environmental issues.

Other groups showed interest in the wilderness, too. The Boy Scouts were formed in 1910 and the Girl Scouts in 1912. And there was a general increase in park visitors during the first years of the twentieth century, leading the U.S. government to focus more attention on its national parks. In government, the cause of preservation had by then

found one of its greatest champions in President Theodore ("Teddy") Roosevelt.

Roosevelt was a man of remarkable energy and broad interests. A birder, big game hunter, rancher, and natural history writer, he loved the American landscape. He was especially fond of the Great Plains area, in North Dakota, where he owned a cattle ranch. There he was a familiar figure, with his wire-rimmed spectacles and bristly mustache, galloping over the open prairie like any other cowpoke.

When Roosevelt came to the White House in 1901, he became the first preservationist president. He camped out

Long skirts and topcoats apparently didn't keep turn-of-the-century visitors to Yellowstone National Park from enjoying a scramble across a fallen log.

Horseback riding was one of President Theodore ("Teddy") Roosevelt's favorite ways to relax. On the job, he was dedicated to preserving wilderness.

with Muir in Yosemite in 1903, and as a result supported adding the valley to Yosemite National Park. During his administration, Roosevelt created 53 wildlife reserves and 16 national monuments. He also signed bills approving five new national parks. His attitude toward preservation was summed up by his words about the Grand Canyon, uttered on a visit there in 1903. He said, "Do nothing to mar its grandeur. . . . Keep it for your children, your children's children, and all who come after you, as the one great sight which every American should see."

Roosevelt's enthusiasm alone was not enough to create a national park in the Grand Canyon, however. A national park must be created by an act of Congress, not by just one man. But the Enabling Act of 1891 and the Antiquities Act of 1906 had given the president authority of another kind. A president could establish national forest reserves, national monuments, and other protected areas. Therefore, under the Antiquities Act, Roosevelt declared the Grand Canyon a national monument in 1908. (The monument was made a national park in 1919.)

The Antiquities Act was originally intended to protect ancient archeological sites from damage. It was passed by Congress in the same year that Mesa Verde was made a national park. The stone cliff dwellings of Mesa Verde,

Colorado, had survived undisturbed for hundreds of years, since Native American people had built them. Then they were "discovered" in 1888 by Richard Wetherill, whose family had settled on the land nearby. At first, the Wetherills allowed reporters and tourists to go through the ruins and actually sold them the priceless prehistoric pottery, baskets, and arrowheads as souvenirs. Later, they realized the archeological importance of the site and its contents, and stopped giving tours. But even then, looters vandalized the place, using blasting powder to knock down a wall in the beautiful Cliff Palace. The Antiquities Act was designed to outlaw just such destruction. It further allowed the president to proclaim as national monuments sites of natural wonders, such as caves and canyons, and sites of historical interest, such as battlefields and forts.

Once the idea of national parks and monuments was firmly established, more and more were added to the list. But the management and protection of those sites left much to be desired. The parks were still endangered by vandals, careless hikers, and poachers, and by commercial developers such as railroad companies. Some confusion existed because the sites were administered by three separate agencies: the Department of the Interior, the War Department, and the Forest Service within the Department of Agriculture. What was needed was one central agency to supervise all the parks and monuments together.

Responding to suggestions from the Sierra Club and others, in 1916 Congress passed an act creating the National Park Service, a bureau within the Department of the Interior. The service's duties were to regulate the use of the parks and promote the idea that parks are set aside to "conserve the scenery and the natural and historic objects and the wild life therein, and . . . leave them unimpaired for the enjoyment of future generations."

Up until this time, all the national parks and monuments had been established in the West. The newly formed park service now wanted to add lands east of the Mississippi River to the system. But by 1916, most eastern land was too developed to preserve in its natural state. Those areas that did qualify were gradually added to the list.

In 1919, Lafayette (now called Acadia) National Park in Maine became the first park east of the Mississippi. Its champion was a Bostonian named George Bucknam Dorr. The area, a beautiful meeting of rocky mountains and rugged ocean shore, had long attracted tourists and landscape painters. Most of the land was owned by private individuals. On scenic Mount Desert Island, many wealthy people had built magnificent summer homes. George Dorr, a millionaire, donated parts of his land that were still in a natural condition and convinced others to do the same. The biggest donor was John D. Rockefeller, Jr., who contributed about a third of the land, more than 11,000 acres.

Camping out 1930s-style in Acadia National Park called for proper clothes and a clean face to start the day. Acadia was the first park east of the Mississippi.

The government had always depended on such donations to acquire land for parks and monuments. Unless the lands were already federally owned, or were transferred from state ownership, this was the only way it could be done. Some parks, such as the Great Smoky Mountains National Park in Tennessee and North Carolina (created in 1926), were funded by people who gave the government money to buy the land. But not only the wealthy gave: thousands of average citizens also made donations.

Schoolchildren collected pennies and nickels to help save the green, forested mountains from the lumber companies' mills. It wasn't until 1961 that the federal government actually paid out some of its own money to buy parkland. Then, it spent $16 million to buy the land for the Cape Cod National Seashore in Massachusetts.

Some of the most recent additions to the National Park System have been in Alaska. America's last frontier contains more than half of the nearly 80 million acres in the system. Early exploration of the Alaskan wilderness by Muir and others made it clear that here was magnificent land, as yet unspoiled, to be preserved. A few Alaskan parks and monuments were designated over the years, but there were disputes among the state and federal governments, industry, and resident Native Americans over how the land should be used.

By the 1920s, many parks, such as California's Sequoia National Park, were overrun with tourists in their newfangled automobiles.

In 1980, Congress passed the Alaska National Interest Lands Conservation Act, which added many acres to the existing parks in the state and created new parks comprising millions of acres. In spite of opposition from mining and oil interests, the preservationists won out. In at least some areas the law allows for nonwasteful use of natural resources by Native American peoples and non-native residents. Although the law didn't make anybody completely happy, a great deal of some of the world's most spectacular scenery was saved.

As more and more parks are created, more and more people visit them. Many people go to camp and hike in the backcountry, in true John Muir style.

But many others prefer to travel by car and to camp where they can drive in. In fact, the American pleasure in automobile travel, and the resulting increase in building roads and hotels, has threatened the quiet purity of the parks for most of this century. It is difficult to balance people's desire for convenience and comfort with the needs of the animals and plants in these delicate natural environments.

The parks that many people have worked and fought to create are now ours to enjoy, but also to watch over and protect. How we enjoy and protect the parks — the subject of the following two chapters — will determine their fate for generations to come.

At One with Nature

Have you ever pushed a canoe out onto a lonely little lake and felt the utter stillness as you realized that you and your companions were the only people there? Or reached a rocky mountaintop, gasping for breath, and felt suddenly dizzy at the vastness of the land spread below you?

When you are far from "civilization," you can *feel* the presence of the land around you. All the sights and sounds, even the air, fill you up from top to toe. Then you begin to understand the experience of the first people to see this land: the Native Americans and the European pioneers who came after them. When you take time to really know our national parks, you will feel that the land is fresh and new, even though others may have come that way before you.

There are as many ways to explore our parks as there are people to explore them. You may be a champion hiker, strong enough to reach that mountaintop. Or you may be a "watcher" who likes to soak up the feeling of a place by sitting quietly and becoming a part of the scene. Perhaps you like to learn about the natural history of a place — how the rocks were formed or what plants have grown there over the centuries. Or maybe you like to identify the birds and animals you see, and keep a record of your discoveries.

Our national parks are the perfect places to do all of these things and more. Depending on your time, skills, and interests, you can learn about and enjoy the parks in a hundred different ways.

For many people, experiencing a park begins with a car trip. You and your family will probably get to the park by car from wherever you live. Once there, you can usually drive right into the park. Although just driving through won't

32

Dawn reveals the peace and solitude of the unspoiled waters of Voyageurs National Park, far north in the Minnesota woods.

really put you in touch with what's special about a park, it's useful for a quick survey at the beginning of your stay.

Many of the roads through our national parks are among the world's most spectacular drives. Going-to-the-Sun Road in Montana's Glacier National Park, for example, offers breathtaking views of snow-white mountains, shimmering lakes, and waterfalls at every turn. Virginia's beautiful Skyline Drive, in Shenandoah National Park, winds through forests that are a fairyland of white blossoms in spring and ablaze with red and yellow leaves in autumn. And a drive to the top of Hawaii's Hale-

Brilliant colors dazzle visitors traveling along Shenandoah National Park's Skyline Drive on a crisp autumn day.

akala Volcano provides sweeping views of the enormous Haleakala Crater, as well as of the land and sea for miles around.

A quick drive-through is as much as many tourists see of our parks. But to really experience a park, you must stay for at least a few days, and preferably longer. Your family may decide to stay in one of the hotels or cabins maintained inside the park, or in a motel just outside its boundaries. But a quicker way to get right into the outdoor spirit, and have fun besides, is to camp out. Sleeping in a tent, or out in the open under a starry sky, puts you directly in touch with your surroundings.

Camping out can be as "civilized" or as primitive as you choose. In most parks, you have several choices. At "improved" campsites, you can drive in with your supplies and equipment. Your campsite will have a cleared area for your tent, a firepit, and access to running water and public rest rooms. "Walk-in" campsites are for people who like to pack in their supplies a short distance but don't want to take a long backpacking trip. These can be reached by a short hike and usually have a cleared area with a firepit and perhaps water. Finally, for dedicated backpackers, there are primitive backcountry campsites, far from the world of cars and people. To camp there, you must pack in everything, including water or equipment for sterilizing stream water.

Once you're at your destination, your activities will be determined by the kind of terrain in the park, its climate, and the available facilities, as well as by your own skills and interests. If you did some research before you left home, you probably already have some idea of what the park has to offer. (A letter to the park before your visit usually brings an envelope stuffed with helpful maps and information.) Even if you didn't do advance research, it's easy to ask the park rangers what activities and facilities are available. A little time spent in the Visitor Center found at most parks will also help get you started.

You'll find that the rangers are your keys to learning about and enjoying the park during your stay. In their familiar green uniforms and Stetson hats, these professionals know the park inside and out. They can tell you about weather conditions, trails, and facilities. They also conduct special guided hikes and tours, as well as campfire talks and programs.

The rangers are the guardians of the park, too. They enforce certain rules that all visitors must follow, both for their own safety and out of respect for the land and its animals and plants. When you visit a national park, you must do all you can to preserve the special peace and quiet of your surroundings. Show your respect for the land by leaving plants and animals alone. Your goal should be to leave the land exactly as you found it, clean and free of litter, and unscarred by careless campfire use.

One activity you can enjoy in almost any park is hiking or walking. And because each park is unique, no two hikes will be quite the same. A hike along the misty coastline of Olympic National Park in Washington state can be leisurely and almost magical. On the beach, you stop to look into tidepools for starfish and sea urchins. Then you turn into the green forest and enter a cool, silent world wrapped in fog.

A hike in Utah's hot, dry Bryce Canyon National Park is an entirely different experience. As you huff and puff along a steep and winding desert trail, you pass weird rock formations with names like Palace of the Fairy Queen and Ruins of Athens. Little lizards called skinks dart across your path, and red-tailed hawks circle above in the clear blue sky.

Hikes can be easy or challenging, hour-long or overnight, independent or guided. Most parks maintain a variety of trails and will provide you with maps and information. In Glacier National Park, for example, there are 800 miles of trails. These range from an easy half-mile walk — from Going-to-the-Sun Road to Avalanche Gorge — to a backpacker's 17-mile loop through the high country, requiring 2 or 3 days' hiking and overnight camping.

Some parks are easy to get around in, while others are true wilderness parks, difficult or impossible to see without backpacking in overnight. An example of each type can be found in Arches National Park and Canyonlands National Park, both near the town of Moab in Utah. Arches contains the largest known collection of natural stone arches in the world. The awesome bridges, towers, and arches of stone were formed by millions of years of erosion. This park is easy to get to and to see; paved roads lead past or near the most interesting rock formations. The trails in the park can all be walked in a day or less.

Nearby Canyonlands, on the other hand, is more of a challenge. Few good roads lead into this vast wilderness, and from them you can get only a hint of the tens of thousands of brightly colored spires, needles, natural arches, and other rock shapes that make the park unique. To see the most remote areas of the park, you would have to take a backpacking trip of several days. Horseshoe Canyon, which contains some of the nation's most mysterious ancient rock paintings, *can* be reached in a four-wheel-drive vehicle. But it must creep slowly down a steep canyon wall while someone walks ahead and removes fallen rocks from the roadbed. You need plenty of wilderness know-how to explore this fascinating desert environment.

Although you can hike many park trails independently, with your family and companions, it's especially interesting to take the hikes guided by a park ranger. This lets you explore areas that are off-limits otherwise, and helps you learn more about what you're seeing. In Kentucky's Mammoth Cave National Park, for example, the only way to visit the caves is on a ranger-guided tour. The amazing mineral formations inside

A tour of Mammoth Cave leads visitors past an eerie rock formation called Frozen Niagara, which seems to plunge toward Crystal Lake, 60 feet below.

Rafting on the waters of Grand Teton National Park's Snake River provides lots of fun in a beautiful, mountain-crowned setting.

them are far too delicate to risk the damage that could be done by unaccompanied visitors. One especially exciting tour, limited to just a few people at a time, leads visitors hiking and crawling on hands and knees through 5 miles of dark passages.

In an area of Arches National Park called the Fiery Furnace, a tricky route leads through a maze of rock that hides 18 stone arches and a natural stone bridge. There you need to take the 2-hour ranger-guided tour just to find your way through! On all guided tours, the rangers will tell you about the plants, animals, rock formations, and other features you are seeing.

In many parks, water rather than land is the focus of activities. For example, Minnesota's Voyageurs National Park is made up almost entirely of lakes. While paddling a canoe on its blue waters, among the pine-covered islands, you can imagine what the area looked like to its early Native American residents and to the French voyageurs — or fur-trapping explorers — of the early 1800s.

Other waterways invite boating of a different kind. For example, you might float down the Rio Grande between steep canyon walls in Big Bend National Park in Texas. The water there and on other rivers can be lazy and gentle. Or it can be wild, requiring expert handling of a raft or kayak through rocky rapids. On challenging whitewater rivers, people sometimes choose to take group trips organized by private outfitters. The outfitters take care of the whole trip, from expert navigation of the rafts to the preparation of delicious meals. (Some companies also offer other kinds of trips: by horseback, wagon, and so on.)

Some boat trips are guided by park rangers. At tropical Biscayne National Park in Florida, you can look through a glass-bottomed boat at brightly colored fish swimming beneath you. At Oregon's Crater Lake, a 2-hour launch ride takes you onto the lake itself. As you cruise past giant rock formations, a ranger tells you about the lake's natural history.

Of course, many parks offer opportunities to get right into the water instead of boating on it. You can snorkel among Biscayne's coral reefs, or swim at many of our beautiful seashores, such as North Carolina's Cape Lookout National Seashore. National lakes and recreation areas also provide a variety of settings for swimming.

If horseback riding appeals to you, the parks provide varied opportunities. You can ride along beautiful wooded trails at Acadia National Park in Maine and at Kings Canyon National Park in California. For a unique experience, you can even take a hair-raising mule trek down into the Grand Canyon. The sure-footed animals carry their riders around hairpin turns that hang out over empty space — not a trip for the faint-hearted!

All of the activities mentioned so far are summertime ones, but in winter many parks are transformed into snowy wonderlands, to be explored in

Curious elk watch as a lone cross-country skier glides quietly through the snowy woods in Yellowstone National Park.

new ways. In Yellowstone National Park, for example, you can strap on snowshoes or cross-country skis and strike out over a network of beautiful trails. Or you can lace up your ice skates and glide out onto the frozen surface of magnificent Yellowstone Lake. The mountains of California's Lassen Volcanic National Park, Colorado's Rocky Mountain National Park, and several other parks in the system also provide opportunities for downhill skiing.

Most of these ways of enjoying the parks involve vigorous physical activity.

But there are many exceptions. For visitors who are disabled, all but the most remote wilderness parks have special facilities and programs to make their visits enjoyable and interesting. And anyone can certainly learn about and enjoy the parks in more contemplative ways. Try sitting quietly by a hidden woodland stream. Soon you may see colorful dragonflies flitting over the water, or shadowy fish swimming past. As you settle into the quiet, your ears will pick up faint sounds, like the whisper of the wind in the trees or the rustle of insects or tiny animals in the fallen leaves.

Tracing lazy circles on the ice beneath a wide sky is one peaceful way to enjoy winter on Yellowstone Lake.

In environments like Florida's Everglades National Park, you can watch many kinds of beautiful birds, such as graceful great egrets, as you stand beside a still pond at dawn. A slow stroll along a creekside meadow in California's Redwood National Park will reward you with a dazzling display of wildflowers in bloom. Or you can wait at the mouth of New Mexico's Carlsbad Caverns at sundown to see hundreds of thousands of bats swirl out into the darkening sky on their nightly insect hunt.

Whether you are an active participant or a "watcher," many of your most memorable experiences of the parks will be those spent in quiet and solitude. But millions of people visit the most popular parks each year, so you won't always have the place to yourself. And unfortunately, you're most likely to encounter the biggest crowds in the summer, the time students are out of school. But there *are* ways to beat the crowds.

If you must travel to a popular park like the Grand Canyon during the summertime, here's something to try: Instead of spending a hot afternoon surrounded by hundreds of other tourists at the South Rim, get up at dawn one morning. You'll forget your sleepiness in a hurry when you see how hushed and beautiful the canyon is in the early morning light. And even in summer, desert mornings are cool. With an adult companion, start down one of the wide

Yellow mustard and purple lupine bloom in cheerful harmony along Wilson Creek in Redwood National Park.

42

These fantastic rock spires, known as The Needles, are only one of the attractions of Canyonlands National Park, less well known but just as fascinating as the Grand Canyon.

trails that lead into the canyon's depths. You may have the trail all to yourselves. Almost everyone will still be asleep! By the time people begin to arrive in late morning, you and your companion will have had a good 3-hour hike (one hour down, two back up). And you will have seen some of the world's greatest scenery in peace and quiet.

Another way to avoid crowds is to choose a park that's less heavily visited than the Grand Canyon. In 1988 the Grand Canyon reported nearly 4 million visitors. In the same year, Canyonlands National Park, with scenery just as breathtaking as that of the Grand Canyon, attracted only about 200,000 people. And Isle Royale National Park, a wilderness island in Michigan, reported only about 25,000!

As you'll find, experiencing our national parks close up will never become boring or repetitive. There is always one more lake to paddle across, one more bend in the canyon, one more pass to climb in the high mountains. Although it sometimes takes a little extra effort to get out into nature and really get to know the parks, you will find that it's always worth it. You will be repaid with memories you can take away and treasure for a long time to come.

43

Perfectly reflected in the still waters of Everglades National Park, a lone great egret stands poised like a white statue.

Facing the Future

It's dawn. The sun has not yet risen beyond the mangrove trees at the far end of the pond. But the puffy clouds are turning pink, and their color is reflected in the smooth, shallow water. Everything is quiet. Almost nothing moves in the warm Florida morning.

Suddenly, with a whir of wings, a flock of graceful white birds appears. The birds circle for a few seconds, then drop toward the pond, floating down on broad wings. Their long legs slip into the water with almost no splash. They close their wings around their slender bodies. These are great egrets, and they have come to hunt for fish and other small creatures that live in the pond.

Other birds join them — two, three, a dozen at a time. Soon the pond is filled with more than a hundred birds. Most are egrets, but a few pelicans appear, too, as well as roseate spoonbills with brilliant pink wings.

This lovely scene is in Everglades National Park, near the southern tip of Florida. Like other parks, Everglades contains something that we want to preserve for the future — the thousands of beautiful birds that make the park unique. But even though this scene is peaceful, Everglades is one of the most threatened of our national parks. Although there appear to be countless birds there, old-timers can tell you that there are far fewer than in days past.

Today the bird population is threatened by water use outside of the park. For many years, an enormous amount of water has been diverted from Everglades and other South Florida areas for agricultural and other uses. As a result, the population of wading birds, including egrets, herons, and others, has steadily declined. In particular, the wood stork, a large wading bird that was once common in the area, is disappearing. It

45

refuses to nest if there is not enough water to meet its need for fish. People in Florida are now taking steps to restore the flow of water into the parks. But there are still no guarantees that the bird population will be fully restored.

Our national lands are threatened in many ways. Human activities within and outside of their boundaries threaten their ecosystems — the delicate, natural balance of land, water, wildlife, and plants. Just because an area is designated a national park, monument, or historic site, it's not automatically protected forever. People concerned with the preservation of our land must always be ready to protect the parks from present and future dangers.

As the example of Everglades National Park illustrates, developments just beyond park boundaries need constant watching. But water diversion is not the only problem. Often, logging, mining, or oil and gas drilling are allowed on federal lands just outside of the parks, on property managed by the Forest Service or other government agencies rather than by the Park Service.

In Olympic National Forest, which surrounds Washington state's Olympic National Park, heavy logging is permitted. As the native western redcedar trees are cut down, the forests are replanted with Douglas fir. These trees are more profitable, because they will grow faster and be ready for cutting sooner. But replacing the native trees will create a single-species forest. In such an environment, native wildlife such as the spotted owl can no longer live. The loggers' pollution of the rivers that flow into the park will also disturb other wild animals such as elk, otter, and fish that migrate along the rivers. So even though trees are not actually being cut inside the park, the animals and waters of the park will still be affected.

Development *within* the parks is an even more dramatic and immediate threat. Proposed dams, in particular, have been a special problem for several parks. The first battle over a dam in a national park concerned California's Yosemite National Park, early in this century. The city of San Francisco wanted to dam the Tuolumne River. The idea was to flood the park's beautiful Hetch Hetchy Valley, creating a reservoir to provide drinking water for the rapidly growing city.

John Muir, Yosemite's leading defender, was outraged. He argued that Hetch Hetchy was as lovely as Yosemite Valley itself. Though he fought hard to defend the valley, Congress approved the dam in 1913. Muir died shortly thereafter, deeply disappointed over the decision. But this cloud of defeat had a silver lining. The dispute was the first major confrontation between conservationists and politicians. A lot of people across the nation had followed the debate. They now saw that it was important to protect the parks from any further damage, and the conservation movement gained many supporters.

Again, in 1963, the U.S. government announced that two dams would be built

Once, lovely Hetch Hetchy Valley (top) was compared in beauty to Yosemite Valley. In 1923, it was hidden under water forever when the Tuolumne River was dammed to create a reservoir (bottom).

in the Grand Canyon. The purpose was to provide more water to the Southwest, where the population was growing rapidly. The dams were to flood almost 150 miles of the Colorado River inside the canyon. Behind the dams, the river that had been carving the gorge for millions of years would flow no more.

By this time, conservationists had had experience in fighting such a proposal. In the 1950s, national and local organizations, including the Sierra Club, distributed literature and wrote letters to Congress to oppose the damming of a Green River canyon inside Dinosaur National Monument. Their efforts had been a success.

Now the Sierra Club took out full-page newspaper ads opposing the damming of the Grand Canyon. One said, in part, ". . . there is only one simple, incredible issue here: this time it's the Grand Canyon they want to flood. *The Grand Canyon!*" The result was a blizzard of letters from the public to Congress, opposing the dams. With the public behind them, the conservationists refused to compromise. Neither dam was built.

Sometimes threats to parks come from apparently innocent sources: plants or animals that people have introduced into a park. When plants or animals become established in an area where they do not occur naturally, they can affect the ecosystem in unexpected ways. For example, the tamarisk (or salt cedar), a bushy tree native to Europe and Asia, was introduced to the Southwest around 1900. This thirsty plant consumes a lot of water, and water is precious in the dry southwestern climate. Now it has crowded out the region's original plants, which used up less water.

In a very different environment — cool, green Olympic National Park in Washington state — white mountain goats range throughout the high country. The goats were introduced into the area for hunting in the 1920s, before the park was established. Now tourists love to see them on the mountainsides, but the goats have done a lot of damage to the park, munching on native wildflowers and other plants. They also roll on the ground in a way that damages the soil. The Park Service is still trying to figure out what to do about the goats.

Another danger to the parks is the very people who visit and enjoy them. Of course, hikers who litter, start fires through carelessness, or create sanitation problems are obvious culprits. And even worse, some visitors deliberately vandalize the parks. Over the years, tourists in Petrified Forest National Park have walked off with irreplaceable pieces of petrified wood. In 1980, vandals in Arches National Park damaged priceless rock paintings left by Native Americans many centuries ago.

But often people damage the parks without meaning to, just by being there. More and more people crowd into our parks every year. While it's wonderful that so many appreciate our parks, they're in danger of being "loved to death." Some hiking trails are so deeply worn that they have become ruts. Water

48

Snowy mountain goats make a dramatic picture against the rocky mountainsides of Olympic National Park. Unfortunately, they cause damage to the park's vegetation and soil.

then drains into the ruts and flows as if in a creek, causing erosion problems. In the more populated parts of the parks, cars contribute their noise and fumes. And the peace of the Grand Canyon is shattered by 50,000 over-flights a year by helicopters and planes.

Although the parks *are* for people, the Park Service is now trying to maintain them in ways that respect and pre-serve the land, animals, and plants. In the old days, park employees often went out of their way to entertain tourists. Spotlights were turned on at night to illuminate Old Faithful geyser in Yellowstone. On summer nights in Yosemite, rangers set a bonfire and pushed it over the edge of 3,000-foot cliff as a "show" for spectators in the valley below. Wild animals were chained near hotels in some parks. Bears were even encouraged to raid garbage dumps at campgrounds so that visitors could see them up close! This disastrous policy turned the bears into aggressive beggars. Some attacked tourists and had to be shot.

Today, visitors are asked to accept the parks for what they are, and to seek out their scenic beauty and wildlife in ways that preserve their precious resources. The Park Service keeps looking for ways to let visitors enjoy themselves without

causing damage. Some parks, such as Yosemite, have restricted the use of cars. Shuttle buses provide a way to tour the valley. In the backcountry, the number of backpackers permitted on the trails at any one time is restricted.

Setting aside true wilderness areas has become an important issue in recent decades. As a result of the Wilderness Act, which Congress passed in 1964, millions of acres are being set aside across the country. Here, by the law's definition, humans are only temporary

In the 1940s, rangers in Yosemite National Park used scraps of food to lure bears out of the backcountry so tourists could get a closer look.

guests. In these areas, no permanent roads or motor vehicles are permitted, and visitors must leave no trace of their presence, aside from the hiking trail itself. Many of these official wilderness areas are inside the parks; others are on land controlled by the U.S. Forest Service and the U.S. Bureau of Land Management.

Adding to the size of our parks is another important way to help preserve them. The National Parks and Conservation Association has recommended that 10 million acres be added to existing National Park System holdings. Also suggested are new national parks and 46 new historic sites. For example, attempts are being made to save a small portion of the original prairie land that once covered most of the Midwest. And a proposal has been put forward to create a Mojave National Park in southern California before the fragile desert ecology is ruined by off-road vehicles and vandals.

Although it takes an act of Congress to establish and preserve a national park, the people who really make it happen are concerned citizens. That means members of environmental organizations such as the Wilderness Society, the Sierra Club, and the Audubon Society, as well as just plain interested individuals. History has taught us that, in the conservation movement, no victories are ever final. Battles that have been "won" by one generation may need to be fought again by the next. And every battle is important, because once it has been lost — once the outstanding feature of a park has been dammed, paved over, or otherwise changed — the park almost never can be restored to its original beauty.

The U.S. National Park System has been a model for all the world. The magnificent Rocky Mountains peaks and the gentle Shenandoah forests, the Everglades birds and the Yellowstone bison, the California redwoods and the southwestern cacti — all are preserved because people have dedicated their time and energy to this important cause. The parks are ours to enjoy, but they are also ours to protect. Their future is in *our* hands.

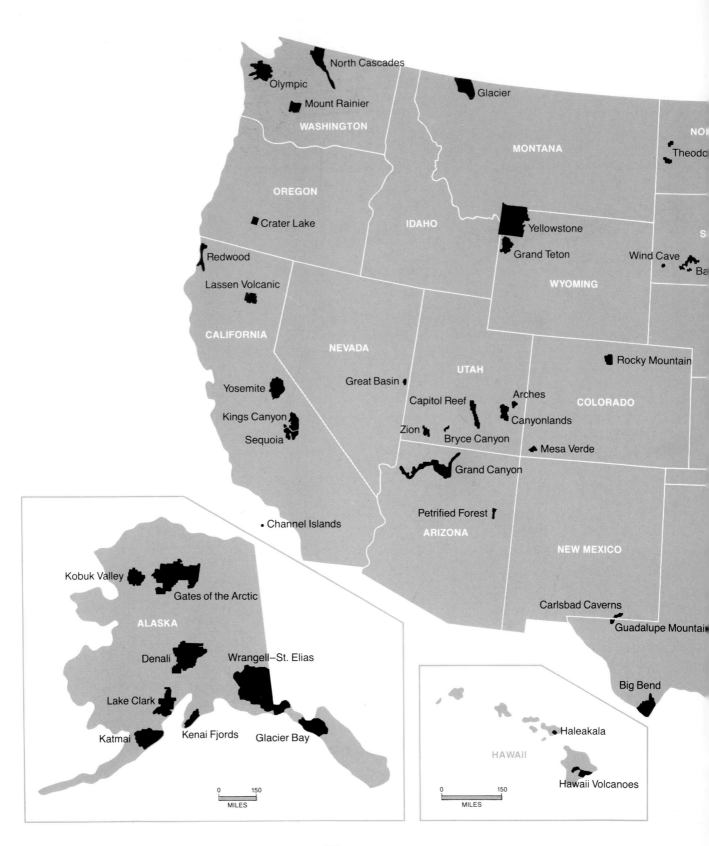

North Cascades

Olympic

Mount Rainier

WASHINGTON

Glacier

MONTANA

NO

Theodo

OREGON

Crater Lake

IDAHO

Yellowstone

Grand Teton

WYOMING

Wind Cave

S

Ba

Redwood

Lassen Volcanic

CALIFORNIA

NEVADA

UTAH

Rocky Mountain

Great Basin

Capitol Reef

Arches

COLORADO

Yosemite

Kings Canyon

Zion

Canyonlands

Sequoia

Bryce Canyon

Mesa Verde

Grand Canyon

Petrified Forest

Channel Islands

ARIZONA

NEW MEXICO

Carlsbad Caverns

Guadalupe Mountain

Kobuk Valley

Gates of the Arctic

ALASKA

Denali

Wrangell–St. Elias

Big Bend

Lake Clark

Katmai

Kenai Fjords

Glacier Bay

Haleakala

HAWAII

Hawaii Volcanoes

0   150
MILES

0   150
MILES

U.S. National Parks

MAINE

Acadia •

DAKOTA

Voyageurs

Isle Royale •

oosevelt

MINNESOTA

VT.

N.H.

H DAKOTA

WISCONSIN

NEW YORK

MASS.

CONN.

R.I.

ds

MICHIGAN

N.J.

IOWA

BRASKA

ILLINOIS

OHIO

PENNSYLVANIA

MARYLAND

DEL.

INDIANA

WEST
VIRGINIA

Shenandoah

KANSAS

MISSOURI

KENTUCKY

VIRGINIA

• Mammoth Cave

Great Smoky Mountains

NORTH CAROLINA

OKLAHOMA

ARKANSAS

TENNESSEE

SOUTH CAROLINA

• Hot Springs

GEORGIA

ALABAMA

MISSISSIPPI

TEXAS

FLORIDA

LOUISIANA

0   150
|___|___|
MILES

Everglades • Biscayne

Outside of map area: National Park of American Samoa and Virgin Islands National Park.

U.S. National Parks

Acadia National Park
MAINE

AREA: 65 square miles

FEATURES: A rocky granite coastline meets the salty tides of the Atlantic Ocean. Many marine animals live in the tidal zones. Above, forests of evergreen and sugar maples, which turn brilliant red in autumn, are home for white-tailed deer, red foxes, and many kinds of birds.

ACTIVITIES: Hiking, backpacking, camping, horseback riding, bicycling, swimming, birding, fishing, cross-country skiing

Arches National Park
UTAH

AREA: 115 square miles

FEATURES: Nearly 100 natural stone arches and thousands of stone spires look bright red at sunrise and sunset. The rugged high-desert scenery, mostly wilderness, is set against a backdrop of snow-capped peaks.

ACTIVITIES: Hiking, backpacking, camping

Badlands National Park
SOUTH DAKOTA

AREA: 380 square miles

FEATURES: Odd-shaped hills and cliffs look like a moonscape. Herds of pronghorn antelope and bison roam across prairie grasslands. Rocks contain fossils of turtles, early horses, and rhinoceros more than 25 million years old.

ACTIVITIES: Hiking, backpacking, camping, horseback riding

Big Bend National Park
TEXAS

AREA: 1,254 square miles

FEATURES: A big bend in the Rio Grande, which forms the boundary betwen Texas and Mexico, gives this desert-and-river park its name. The deep river canyon contains fossils of marine creatures and dinosaurs. Bright fields of desert wildflowers and nearly 400 different kinds of birds — more than in any other park — are other attractions.

ACTIVITIES: Hiking, backpacking, camping, horseback riding, river float trips, fishing, birding

Biscayne National Park
FLORIDA

AREA: 270 square miles (7 square miles of land)

FEATURES: Although it contains 44 islands, 95 percent of the park is underwater. Snorkelers swim with dolphins and brilliantly colored fish through magical coral reefs. Pirates once hid in creeks and bays here to attack ships loaded with silver cargo.

ACTIVITIES: Hiking, backpacking, camping, snorkeling, scuba diving, swimming, boating, fishing

Bryce Canyon National Park
UTAH

AREA: 56 square miles

FEATURES: Thousands of strangely shaped pink and orange spires line the sides of a deep amphitheater. Higher up, mule deer wander through forests of colorful "quaking" aspen. Ancient bristlecone pines have survived here for as long as 1,700 years.

ACTIVITIES: Hiking, backpacking, camping, cross-country skiing

Canyonlands National Park
UTAH

AREA: 527 square miles

FEATURES: Two mighty rivers meet between steep canyon walls, producing whitewater rapids as well as calmer stretches of water. The park contains one of the world's greatest displays of unusual rock formations and mysterious rock paintings by ancient peoples.

ACTIVITIES: Hiking, backpacking, camping, fishing, river trips

Capitol Reef National Park
UTAH

AREA: 378 square miles

FEATURES: Looking like an ocean reef, the rock layers of the Waterpocket Fold have been pushed up to form cliffs which tower above the neighboring earth. Indians called one part of these colorful cliffs the "Sleeping Rainbow." In Cathedral Valley, majestic rock formations rise hundreds of feet from the desert floor.

ACTIVITIES: Hiking, backpacking, camping

Carlsbad Caverns National Park
NEW MEXICO

AREA: 73 square miles

FEATURES: Passages in this series of underground caves lead to limestone "rooms" filled with stalactites, stalagmites, and crystals. Every summer night, some 300,000 bats fly out of the cavern to hunt insects. Bat fossils are also found within the caves.

ACTIVITIES: Hiking, backpacking, cavern touring, nature walks, bat flight program

Channel Islands National Park
CALIFORNIA

AREA: 389 square miles (198 square miles of land)

FEATURES: Five mountainous islands off Santa Barbara are carpeted with millions of wildflowers each spring. Migrating gray whales swim past in search of food every winter. Pelicans nose-dive into the ocean after fish, and bellowing elephant seals entertain human visitors in the springtime.

ACTIVITIES: Hiking, backpacking, camping, birding, sea mammal watching, scuba diving, swimming, fishing

Crater Lake National Park
OREGON

AREA: 286 square miles

FEATURES: Almost 7,000 years ago, a huge volcano erupted. Its top collapsed into the empty hole left by the eruption. Over time, a beautiful dark blue lake — the deepest in the United States — filled the rest of the hole.

ACTIVITIES: Hiking, backpacking, camping, cross-country skiing, snowshoeing, horseback riding, boat tours

Denali National Park and Preserve
ALASKA

AREA: 9,419 square miles

FEATURES: At 20,320 feet above sea level, Mount McKinley is North America's tallest mountain. It is always covered with snow. Caribou, grizzly bear, wolves, moose, and sheep roam the vast, open, almost treeless landscape.

ACTIVITIES: Hiking, backpacking, camping, cross-country skiing, advanced mountain climbing, bus tours for wildlife viewing

Everglades National Park
FLORIDA

AREA: 2,185 square miles

FEATURES: Through a sweeping, open, flat land of prairie grass, pine trees, and swamps, water flows slowly to the sea. Big beautiful birds — herons, egrets, storks, pelicans, spoonbills — come here by the thousands to hunt fish. And alligators prey on anything they can.

ACTIVITIES: Hiking, backpacking, camping, boating, birding, bicycling, fishing, guided boat trips

Gates of the Arctic National Park and Preserve
ALASKA

AREA: 13,238 square miles

FEATURES: Two huge peaks guard one route up a deep valley to true adventure. Here you are on your own in a wilderness without trails, signs, or telephones! Entirely above the Arctic Circle, this is the northernmost park in the system.

ACTIVITIES: Hiking, restricted backpacking and camping, cross-country skiing, mountain climbing, float trips, birding, fishing, kayaking

Glacier Bay National Park and Preserve
ALASKA

AREA: 5,130 square miles

FEATURES: A rapidly melting glacier is retreating farther north each year. It leaves a deep bay behind, which can be explored by boat. Huge chunks of ice snap off the glacier and crash into the bay regularly.

ACTIVITIES: Hiking, backpacking, camping, guided boat trips, canoeing, kayaking, fishing, mountain climbing, cross-country skiing, whale watching

Glacier National Park
MONTANA

AREA: 1,584 square miles

FEATURES: In the high mountain country of the northern Rockies, this park meets a Canadian park at the border. Glaciers carved its deep valleys, and in fact, 50 small glaciers still remain in the highest valleys. In the fall, large numbers of bald and golden eagles arrive to feed on salmon.

ACTIVITIES: Hiking, backpacking, camping, birding, cross-country skiing, horseback riding, boating, fishing, bicycling

Grand Canyon National Park
ARIZONA

AREA: 1,903 square miles

FEATURES: This gorge carved by the Colorado River is one of the world's greatest wonders. From the top of the canyon to the bottom, four life zones — from desert to pine forest — can be seen. Two billion years of earth's geological history are there for us to read in the many layers of rock.

ACTIVITIES: Hiking, backpacking, camping, mule trips, river raft tours

Grand Teton National Park
WYOMING

AREA: 485 square miles

FEATURES: Jagged snowy mountain peaks rise high into the sky just west of the Great Plains. Far below them, the Snake River winds across the broad flat valley called Jackson Hole. Herds of elk and moose, as well as other wildlife, share the peaceful valley and its lakes.

ACTIVITIES: Hiking, backpacking, camping, horseback riding, mountain climbing, float trips, fishing, cross-country skiing

Great Basin National Park
NEVADA

AREA: 120 square miles

FEATURES: Huge glaciers carved out this landscape. Up near the timberline, bristlecone pine trees, twisted by the wind, are several thousand years old. The Lehman Caves contain stalactites, stalagmites, and gigantic narrow columns in many colors.

ACTIVITIES: Hiking, backpacking, camping, cave exploration, cross-country skiing

Great Smoky Mountains National Park
NORTH CAROLINA AND TENNESSEE

AREA: 813 square miles

FEATURES: In summer, in the loveliest mountains of the East, a smoky haze covers the land. The hills are pink with rhododendron blossoms in spring, and red and gold in the fall. Black bears rule the woods here.

ACTIVITIES: Hiking, backpacking, camping, horseback riding, bicycling, fishing, cross-country skiing, sledding, tobogganing

Guadalupe Mountains National Park
TEXAS

AREA: 135 square miles

FEATURES: Once a reef, or shelf, in a prehistoric sea, these mountains are now surrounded by desert. At their tops are cool forests, however, and natural springs create oases even at the desert level.

ACTIVITIES: Hiking, backpacking, camping

Haleakala National Park
HAWAII

AREA: 44 square miles

FEATURES: This park of great contrasts includes the weird, moonlike landscape of a volcanic crater. The park continues down the side of the volcano through a tropical rain forest valley, and ends at sea level on the beautiful Maui coast.

ACTIVITIES: Hiking, backpacking, camping, horseback riding, swimming

Hawaii Volcanoes National Park
HAWAII

AREA: 358 square miles

FEATURES: Within this park on the big island of Hawaii are two very active volcanoes: Kilauea and Mauna Loa. At both, you can hike up to see the lava flows. Some lucky visitors even watch actual eruptions.

ACTIVITIES: Hiking, backpacking, camping

Hot Springs National Park
ARKANSAS

AREA: 9 square miles

FEATURES: Thousands of gallons of hot (143°F) water flow daily from 47 natural hot springs. Visitors bathe in the water in handsome old bathhouses, seeking relief from pain, cures for ailments, and just relaxation. The springs are surrounded by beautiful woodlands.

ACTIVITIES: Hiking, backpacking, camping, horseback riding, swimming, boating, hot springs bathing

Isle Royale National Park
MICHIGAN

AREA: 893 square miles

FEATURES: This wilderness island on chilly Lake Superior is just 15 miles from Canada. At the turn of the century, moose swam over to populate it. They were followed at mid-century by wolves, who crossed on ice to prey on them.

ACTIVITIES: Hiking, backpacking, camping, boating, canoeing

Katmai National Park and Preserve
ALASKA

AREA: 6,391 square miles

FEATURES: In 1912, one of history's largest volcanic eruptions resulted in the collapse of the dome of Mount Katmai. Ash was spread across 1,500 miles, creating the Valley of Ten Thousand Smokes. In this weird but beautiful landscape, astronauts practiced for landings on the moon.

ACTIVITIES: Hiking, backpacking, camping, boating, fishing, float trips, canoeing, kayaking, bus tours

Kenai Fjords National Park
ALASKA

AREA: 1,047 square miles

FEATURES: This coastline park is half ice field, half alternating fingers of ocean and land. Seals, sea otters, and hundreds of thousands of birds crowd the rugged coastline and dot the offshore islands.

ACTIVITIES: Hiking, backpacking, camping, birding, cross-country skiing, fishing, advanced mountain climbing, boat tours for wildlife viewing

Kings Canyon National Park
CALIFORNIA

AREA: 721 square miles

FEATURES: With more than 8,000 feet from the top ridge to the river below, Kings Canyon is the deepest gorge in North America. Crossed by raging rivers and studded with lakes, this is a true wilderness park.

ACTIVITIES: Hiking, backpacking, camping, horseback riding, cross-country skiing, fishing, mountain climbing

Kobuk Valley National Park
ALASKA

AREA: 2,735 square miles

FEATURES: Twice yearly, thousands of caribou migrate through Kobuk Valley, north of the Arctic Circle. Native Americans have hunted them for 12,500 years. The Kobuk River flows past an arctic desert whose huge sand dunes look like waves.

ACTIVITIES: Hiking, backpacking, camping, fishing, float trips, birding

Lake Clark National Park and Preserve
ALASKA

AREA: 6,319 square miles

FEATURES: Here is a complete geographical assortment: mountains, glaciers, two active volcanoes, deep valleys, alpine meadows, and coastal beaches. Millions of bright red salmon come to huge Lake Clark and its streams each year to lay their eggs.

ACTIVITIES: Hiking, backpacking, camping, climbing, rafting, kayaking, fishing, boating

Lassen Volcanic National Park
CALIFORNIA

AREA: 166 square miles

FEATURES: Spectacular volcanic eruptions from 1914 to 1917 excited America and led to the creation of this park. Today the restless land still produces boiling springs, bubbling mudpots, and hot, hissing steam that rises from cracks in the ground.

ACTIVITIES: Hiking, backpacking, camping, swimming, fishing, boating, downhill and cross country skiing

Mammoth Cave National Park
KENTUCKY

AREA: 81 square miles

FEATURES: The world's largest known underground cave system has more than 330 miles of mapped passages. Probably more remain to be discovered in it. Because eyes and colors would be useless in the darkness of the caves, blind and colorless fish, shrimp, and spiders have evolved there.

ACTIVITIES: Hiking, backpacking, camping, fishing, boating, cave exploration

Mesa Verde National Park
COLORADO

AREA: 81 square miles

FEATURES: The park preserves an ancient Indian city of stone cliff houses. It was mysteriously abandoned 700 years ago, perhaps due to a long drought in the area.

ACTIVITIES: Hiking, backpacking, bicycling

Mount Rainier National Park
WASHINGTON

AREA: 368 square miles

FEATURES: A massive volcano, Mount Rainier is topped with 40 square miles of glaciers. In summer, vast fields of wildflowers appear as the snow melts. For well over 100 years, people have met the physical and mental challenge of climbing the 14,410-foot peak.

ACTIVITIES: Hiking, backpacking, camping, mountain climbing, cross-country skiing, snowshoeing, snow sliding, fishing, boating

National Park of American Samoa
AMERICAN SAMOA

AREA: 13 square miles

FEATURES: Beaches, coral reefs, and rain forests are the main attractions on this lovely island in the South Pacific. The park also protects archeological sites and areas important to the culture of the Samoan people.

ACTIVITIES: Day hiking, swimming, snorkeling, fishing

North Cascades National Park
WASHINGTON

AREA: 788 square miles

FEATURES: Often compared to the Alps, these jagged mountains were carved by glaciers during the Ice Age. Hundreds of miles of trails lead to deep forests, wildflower meadows, waterfalls, and beaver dams. Park animals include mountain lions, bobcats, bears, and mountain goats.

ACTIVITIES: Hiking, backpacking, camping, horseback riding, mountain climbing, cross-country skiing, boating, rafting, fishing

Olympic National Park
WASHINGTON

AREA: 1,429 square miles

FEATURES: The park is divided into three "worlds." From snow-topped mountains, 13 rivers tumble to the sea. The rain forests are dark and mysterious. At the seashore, birds and other creatures share the beach with crashing waves.

ACTIVITIES: Hiking, backpacking, camping, cross-country skiing, mountain climbing, horseback riding, swimming, boating, fishing

Petrified Forest National Park
ARIZONA

AREA: 146 square miles

FEATURES: Millions of years ago, gigantic trees that had fallen and been covered with water began to absorb minerals. In time, they turned to stone. They now lie exposed in a desert, showing their brilliant colors to the sun. The Painted Desert is another attraction of this landscape.

ACTIVITIES: Hiking, backpacking

Redwood National Park
CALIFORNIA

AREA: 172 square miles

FEATURES: In a mysterious, foggy world of heavy rainfall along the Pacific Coast, the great redwoods grow. These are the tallest living things on earth. Elk roam the meadows and the cool, dark forests.

ACTIVITIES: Hiking, camping, horseback riding, swimming, fishing

Rocky Mountain National Park
COLORADO

AREA: 414 square miles

FEATURES: These mountains rise over 14,000 feet. The nation's highest paved highway crosses the park. It passes beaver ponds, snowfields, huge volcanic ashflows, and herds of bighorn sheep. Elk graze the grasslands in huge numbers.

ACTIVITIES: Hiking, backpacking, camping, horseback riding, downhill and cross-country skiing, fishing

Sequoia National Park

CALIFORNIA

AREA: 628 square miles

FEATURES: This is the home of the giant sequoia trees, which can live up to 3,000 years. At one edge of the park stands Mount Whitney, the highest mountain in the United States outside of Alaska. There are spectacular views from the high-country hiking trails.

ACTIVITIES: Hiking, backpacking, camping, snowshoeing, downhill and cross-country skiing, mountain climbing, horseback riding, fishing

Shenandoah National Park

VIRGINIA

AREA: 305 square miles

FEATURES: Dense hardwood forests blanket the Blue Ridge. In the fall, their leaves turn red, orange, and yellow for miles. They can be viewed from above from Skyline Drive, which runs along the top of the ridge.

ACTIVITIES: Hiking, backpacking, camping, horseback riding, bicycling, fishing, cross-country skiing

Theodore Roosevelt National Park

NORTH DAKOTA

AREA: 110 square miles

FEATURES: Roosevelt ranched here as a young man, before he became president. Today, bison, Texas longhorn steers, and wild horses roam through the grasslands and low hills of the "badlands."

ACTIVITIES: Hiking, backpacking, camping, horseback riding, cross-country skiing, canoeing, fishing

Virgin Islands National Park

U.S. VIRGIN ISLANDS

AREA: 23 square miles

FEATURES: Here is a true tropical paradise: lush green hills, white sandy beaches, quiet coves, and blue-green bays for underwater exploration. The park occupies most of the island of St. John and its offshore waters.

ACTIVITIES: Hiking, camping, swimming, scuba diving, snorkeling, boating, fishing

Voyageurs National Park

MINNESOTA

AREA: 341 square miles

FEATURES: A mixture of lake waters, islands, and mainland at the U.S.–Canada border, this land was shaped by glaciers. The park's name honors the French traders who paddled their birchbark canoes through this wilderness to deliver beaver skins to the East Coast.

ACTIVITIES: Hiking, backpacking, camping, swimming, boating, canoeing, fishing, ice fishing, cross-country skiing

Wind Cave National Park

SOUTH DAKOTA

AREA: 44 square miles above ground

FEATURES: This is one of the world's longest and most complex caves. Changes in air pressure send wind whistling in and out of it. Instead of stalactites and stalagmites, these caves feature mineral formations called "popcorn" and "frostwork." Above-ground are grasslands full of prairie dogs and bison.

ACTIVITIES: Hiking, backpacking, camping, cave exploration

Wrangell–St. Elias National Park and Preserve
ALASKA

AREA: 20,607 square miles

FEATURES: In the biggest U.S. park, the world's highest seaside mountains rise 18,000 feet above the Gulf of Alaska. The park also includes North America's two largest glaciers. Everything seems oversize in this spectacular park that demands a visitor's respect.

ACTIVITIES: Hiking, backpacking, and camping with caution; horseback riding, cross-country skiing, mountain climbing, rafting, boating, fishing

Yosemite National Park
CALIFORNIA

AREA: 1,189 square miles

FEATURES: In beautiful Yosemite Valley, waterfalls plunge hundreds of feet down gray granite cliffs to a flat river valley carved by ancient glaciers. The wild higher country provides sweeping views of sunlit peaks, flower-filled meadows, and alpine lakes.

ACTIVITIES: Hiking, backpacking, camping, horseback riding, bicycling, downhill and cross-country skiing, ice skating, swimming, boating, fishing, mountain climbing

Yellowstone National Park
WYOMING, IDAHO, AND MONTANA

AREA: 3,469 square miles

FEATURES: The oldest U.S. park offers all kinds of wilderness beauty: mountains, rivers, forests, lakes, plains, canyons. In addition, it contains 10,000 "thermal features": geysers, mudpots, fumaroles, hot springs. It is home to bears, deer, moose, bighorn sheep, bison, and elk.

ACTIVITIES: Hiking, backpacking, camping, horseback riding, cross-country skiing, boating, fishing

Zion National Park
UTAH

AREA: 229 square miles

FEATURES: This lovely desert canyon and river are lined with high pale sandstone walls, "weeping" rocks, and hanging gardens. To see the awesome 20-foot-wide Narrows, it's necessary to wade through deep waters.

ACTIVITIES: Hiking, backpacking, camping, mountain climbing, horseback riding, cross-country skiing

Index

Acadia National Park, 28–29, 39, 54
Alagnak Wild River, 12
Alaska National Interest Lands Conservation
    Act, 31
Antiquities Act of 1906, 27–28
Appalachian National Scenic Trail, 13
Arches National Park, 1, 36, 39, 48, 54
Audubon Society, 51
Avalanche Gorge, 36

Badlands National Park, 54
Battlefields, national, 13
Bears, 50
Big Bend National Park, 39, 54
Biscayne National Park, 39, 55
Boating, 39
Boy Scouts, 26
Bryce Canyon National Park, 36, 55
Buses, use of in parks, 50

Camping, 35
Canoeing, 39
Canyonlands National Park, 18, 36, 43, 55
Cape Cod National Seashore, 29
Cape Hatteras National Seashore, 12
Cape Lookout National Seashore, 39
Capitol Reef National Park, 55
Carlsbad Caverns National Park, 42, 55
Channel Islands National Park, 55
Cliff Palace, 10, 28
Colorado River, proposed dam for, 46, 48
Colter, John, 18
Crater Lake National Park, 24, 39, 56
Crowds, avoiding, 42–43
Crystal Lake, 37

Dams, 8, 46, 47, 48
Delaware Water Gap National Recreation
    Area, 12
Denali National Park and Preserve, 9, 56
Devil's Tower, 11
Dinosaur National Monument, 12, 48

Disabled, park facilities for, 40
Dorr, George Bucknam, 28
Double Arch, 1
Driving in parks, 32–35

Enabling Act of 1891, 27
Everglades National Park, 11, 42, 44–46, 56

Fiery Furnace, 39
Frozen Niagara, 37

Gates of the Arctic National Park and Preserve,
    56
Gateway National Recreation Area, 13
Girl Scouts, 26
Glacier Bay National Park and Preserve, 9, 56
Glacier National Park, 34, 36, 56
Glen Canyon National Recreation Area, 13
Goats, mountain, 48, 49
Going-to-the-Sun Road, 34, 36
Grand Canyon National Park, 6–8, 17, 27, 39,
    42–43, 48, 49, 57
Grand Teton National Park, 2, 38, 57
Great Basin National Park, 57
Great Smoky Mountains National Park, 29, 57
Green River, proposed dam for, 48
Guadalupe Mountains National Park, 57

Haleakala National Park, 34–35, 57
Hawaii Volcanoes National Park, 9, 11, 58
Hedges, Cornelius, 19
Hetch Hetchy Valley, flooding of, 46–47
Hiking, 35–36, 39
Historical parks, national, 13
Historic sites, national, 13
Horseback riding, 39
Horseshoe Canyon, 36
Hot Springs National Park, 58
Hot Springs Reservation, 18, 19

Ice skating, 40, 41
Isle Royale National Park, 43, 58

Ives, Lt. Joseph, 17

Johnson, Robert Underwood, 23, 24, 25

Katmai National Park and Preserve, 58
Kayaking, 39
Kenai Fjords National Park, 58
Kings Canyon National Park, 39, 58
Kobuk Valley National Park, 59

Lafayette National Park. *See* Acadia National Park
Lake Clark National Park and Preserve, 59
Lakeshores, national, 12
Langford, Nathaniel P., 19
Lassen Volcanic National Park, 40, 59
Logging, 16, 46
Longs Peak, 25

Mammoth Cave National Park, 9, 36–37, 39, 59
McKinley, Mount, 9
Mesa Verde National Park, 10, 11, 27–28, 59
Mills, Enos, 25
Mining, 8, 46
Mojave National Park, proposed, 51
Monuments, national, 11–12
Mount Desert Island, 28
Mount Rainier National Park, 59
Muir, John, 21–24, 25, 27, 30, 46
Mule riding, 39

National Park of American Samoa, 60
National Parks and Conservation Association, 51
The Needles, 43
North Cascades National Park, 60

Old Faithful, 11, 19, 49
Olympic National Park, 8, 36, 46, 48, 49, 60
Organ Pipe Cactus National Monument, 11–12

Palace of the Fairy Queen, 36
Parks, national system of, 8–9, 11, 28–30, 51
Petrified Forest National Park, 48, 60
Pictured Rocks National Lakeshore, 12
Pikes Peak, 25
Powell, Major John Wesley, 17–18
Puu o Keokeo, 9

Rafting, 39

Rangers, 35, 36, 39
Recreation areas, national, 13
Redwood National Park, 9, 42, 60
Rockefeller, John D., Jr., 28
Rocky Mountain National Park, 11, 25, 40, 60
Roosevelt, President Theodore ("Teddy"), 26–27
Ruins of Athens, 36
Russell Cave National Monument, 12

Saint Croix National Scenic Riverway, 12
Scenic trails, national, 12–13
Seashores, national, 12
Sequoia National Park, 30, 61
Shenandoah National Park, 11, 14, 34, 61
Sierra Club, 25–26, 28, 48, 51
Skiing, 40
Skyline Drive, 34
Snake River, 2, 38
Snowshoeing, 40
Statue of Liberty National Monument, 13
Steel, William Gladstone, 24
Swimming, 39

Tamarisk (salt cedar), problem of, 48
Theodore Roosevelt National Park, 61
Thoreau, Henry David, 21
Toroweap Point, 7

Vandalism, 48, 51
Virgin Islands National Park, 61
Voyageurs National Park, 33, 39, 61

Wetherill, Richard, 28
Wild and scenic rivers, national, 12
Wilderness Act, 50
Wilderness Society, 51
Wind Cave National Park, 61
Wood stork, 45–46
Wrangell–St. Elias National Park and Preserve, 62

Yellowstone Lake, 40, 41
Yellowstone National Park, 11, 18–21, 26, 40, 49, 62
Yosemite National Park, 21–24, 25, 27, 46, 49, 50, 62

Zion National Park, 62